The Reduced History of GOLF

First published in 2005 by
Carlton Books Ltd
20 Mortimer Street
London W1T 3JW

Reprinted 2005

A CIP catalogue record of this book is available from the British Library

ISBN 1 86200 228 2

Printed in Singapore

Words: Aubrey Ganguly & Justyn Barnes
Illustrations: Tony Husband
Art Director/Jacket Design: Olly Smee
Photoshop/Design: Martin Dickson
Production: Lisa French
Commissioning Editor: Martin Corteel

The Reduced History of GOLF

The story of the Royal & Ancient game squeezed into 72 holes

Aubrey Ganguly & Justyn Barnes Illustrations by Tony Husband

SEVENOAKS

This book is dedicated to everyone who seeks the meaning of life, golf and George Bush's vocabulary…

INTRODUCTION

Golf, eh? Top hole! And very, very ancient. The glorious idea of trying to hit a small ball into a little hole first emerged nearly 800 years ago.

And what a feather-stuffed, ball-thwacking, wood-wobbling, nation-dividing, trophy-losing, water-hazard-strewn 800 years it's been. Full of presidents and kings, dancing girls and gardeners.

Of course, we know what you're thinking: how could we possibly cram it all into one book – especially, a book as perfectly formed, but, let's face it, small, as this one?

Luckily, dear reader, that was our problem, not yours. We scoured parchments, newspapers and encyclopedias the size of Denmark so that you wouldn't have to.

Instead, sit back, relax and enjoy (very) abbreviated highlights from golf's history, tidily condensed into a casual stroll around 72 holes… plus an old-fashioned 36-hole play-off's worth of moments.

Um… fore!

TEE TIME

1 Who invented golf?!

An in-depth investigation

Deep in the mists of time, golf was invented. Which is fortunate, because otherwise this would have been a very short book. But who did the inventing? Sadly, those pesky mists are too misty for anyone to see through. We think it was the Scots. But it might have been the Dutch. Or the French. Or maybe the Belgians...

One thing we *do* know is that the Scottish have the first records of anyone actually playing golf. But other games may have been forerunners of the sport including *chole*, played in northern France and Belgium; *jeu de maille*, popular with Louis XIV; and *kolven* which was favoured by the Dutch. *Chole* was a cross-country event with the target a distant pillar or door. Unlike golf though, you could hit your opponent's ball. *Jeu de Maille* was even less like golf as we know it, while *kolven* used a ball the size of a cricket ball and was often played on frozen rivers.

All of which leads us to conclude that, er, well, we don't know who invented golf either, but we're very glad they did. Because the reduced history of *kolven* would have been no fun to write...

2 Royals ban ye olde golfe!

Never afraid to annoy the populace, the Royals decreed in the 15th century that golf be banned. Astonishingly, we have found that decree!

By royal decree, this seventeenth day of His Lord's year of fourteen hundred and ninety one, it is pronounced, declared, announced and demanded that His Majesty's subjects should no longer partake in that frankly annoying pastime known as ye olde golfe. Let it be known that any village or towne that plays host to such an event will be denied parsnips, turnips and possibly even potatoes for as long as The King sees fit. Let it also be known that this decree is in no way a sudden response to,or, as some have suggested, another of ye olde hissy fits following our illustrious monarch's recent fourteen attempted shots to get out of a bunker. The actual reasoning behind this decree is of course the wise observation by our kingliness that ye olde golfe is taking up time that thou could better spend battling and fighting with bows, arrows, clubs and swords and the like. So there.
The King

3 Royals love ye olde golfe!

Never afraid to make a U-turn, the Royals decide golf should not be banned. Assassinations and executions were also still popular...

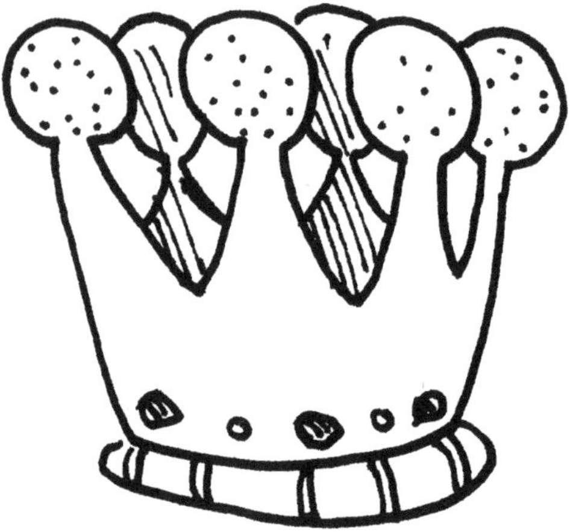

Unlike some of her forebears, Mary Queen of Scots was a fan of golf. So much so that, in 1567, she was seen playing a round shortly after her husband was assassinated. Which some royal-watchers may have perceived as a tad insensitive... especially as her playing partner was the Earl of Bothwell, the prime suspect in the murder. In a trial tagged as "Ye original O.J." (probably) Bothwell was found not guilty. Which was handy, as he then married the Queen.

For some strange reason, Mary's army subsequently deserted her. Defenceless, she threw herself on the mercy of Elizabeth I, was jailed for life and later executed. (Hmm, how merciful...)

More importantly though, golf's popularity continued to flourish. Hooray!

4 St Andrews sets the standard

"The home of golf" gets royal seal of approval

Formed in 1754, and pretty much the oldest course in golf, St Andrews was rather miffed (if a course can be miffed) when the Duke of St Andrews – also known as King William – decided, in 1833, to give the first royal patronage to the Perth Golfing Society.

Later, the King rectified his oversight after he was petitioned to become a St Andrews patron and grant the unique title of Royal and Ancient, which he did in 1834.

Centuries later still, St Andrews continues to be known as "The home of golf" (although you can't play in your slippers there) and challenges visitors with its, er, challenges.

Back in 1885, David Ayrton took an 11 at the 17th hole to lose The Open by two strokes. Eighty-five years later, Doug Sanders lost The Open after taking five at the "easy" 18th.

Sadly, we couldn't find a record of King William's scores, but it's probably safe to assume that he didn't have to buy his own drinks at the 19th hole.

5 Nature and nurture

How early courses were, um, nibbled into shape

Picture the scene... actually, first, turn on your stereo and start playing Edvard Grieg's *Peer Gynt Suite No.1, Morning Mood* (yes, you do know it – it's been in a million ads). Listening? Good. Now picture the scene.

A summer's day. In the distance a wooded hillside bristles and flickers from the cool breeze and the beating sun. Hark! A birdsong! The shrill tune pierces the morning dew. In the long grass we hear rustling. Whose is that face, nose twitching with anticipation? Why, it's a rabbit! Here he comes now, bounding forward, his hind legs just degrees from lop-sided, his ears pinned back by his own pace. Stopping and starting, by turn cautious and carefree as he makes his way towards his target – yes, the greenest grass is always ripest for nibbling! After a quick reconnaissance,

he makes his move. He's not alone. Other animals graze the land, hooves tear holes in the turf to create natural bunkers. The movement of the waters over the ages leavens and shapes the ground, leaving sandy rolling slopes. Our floppy-eared friend continues his feast. And lo – a golf course is formed!

Or, to put it less lyrically, golf courses used to be unkempt and unkept, shaped by nature and grazing animals, and missing such modern luxuries as neatly marked-off tees or clearly defined fairways or greens. Over the years St Andrews and other Scottish courses became more refined and professionally tended. Oh, and the rabbits sought alternative employment in cartoons. (You can turn the music off now...)

6 The Royal & Ancient rules OK!

As courses became more refined, so did the rules of the game. In another of our literally unbelievable exclusives, we've found the minutes from an early rules meeting...

MEETING TO CODIFY RULES OF GOLF
The Royal & Ancient, St Andrews
May 14, 1754

Chairman: JN - Lord. J. Nicklaus
Delegates: SB - Sir S. Ballesteros, NF - Dr N.Faldo, GS - Professor G. Sarazen

MINUTES

TEEING OFF

JN: Suggests that the teeing area should be positioned on the ground.
SB: Asks why can't they be planted in the branches of trees as that would make for a more challenging shot.
NF: Says it doesn't matter where we decide to place the teeing area – the press will distort our decision anyway.
GS: "Good grief."

WATER HAZARDS

SB: Recommends shots are played from wherever they land – even in water. It'll be fun!
JN: Wonders whether it might not be more practical to throw the ball six yards behind the hazard and play from there.
NF: Blames the media for creating the water hazards.
GS: "Good grief."

PUTTING

JN: Offers that the player furthest from the hole should putt first.
NF: Demands that the press not be allowed to look at the green when he's putting.
SB: Suggests everyone should putt before they reach the green. It's more of a challenge!
GS: Announces his resignation from the committee...

7 Ball wars

Featheries v. gutties!

1848 saw a war break out. Well, actually, it saw several – there were revolutions all around Europe. But the war we speak of was between makers of the "feathery" and the "gutty". The what? And, indeed, the what? Let us enlighten you...

In golf's early days, wooden balls were used. But these were soon replaced with featheries, which were made by stuffing a hatful of feathers into a leather casing – a process that required skill and time. Allan Robertson, one of golf's first notable professionals, used to make featheries from his kitchen "factory", helped by his partner Tom Morris. However, the partnership was no more when Robertson discovered Morris playing with – gasp – gutties! Made from the coagulated and moulded juice of the gutta-percha tree, gutties were cheaper and more resilient than featheries. In time they ensured the end of featheries and their lower price helped increase golf's popularity. Robertson, however, died from jaundice before the boom set in. Morris became a greenkeeper and had a son. Whom he named Tom. In war, there are no winners.

8 Brassies, mashies, spoons...

...and other strange names for golf clubs

As time, and the world, moves on, so does language. Words that were once commonplace can now begin to sound a little strange, or perhaps even funny. Presumably, a hundred years from now, terms like "chav", "geek" and "Ronan Keating" will sound bizarre. So it would be somewhat unreasonable for us to ridicule the early names of golf clubs from the 19th century... but yes, we're going to.

A No. 2 wood was originally called a brassie! A No. 5 iron, a mashie! A No. 3 or 4 wood, a spoon! Futher hilarious terms included a cleek, a mashie-niblick and a midmashie!

Sadly, the emergence of the steel shaft in the 1920s and the production of matched sets of clubs ended this tradition of mad names, as clubs began to be known by their numbers. Balderdash!

9 Different strokes

Matchplay is, um, extinguished by the emergence of strokeplay as the championship norm

Let's face it, man is a competitive beast. For all the PC talk of "It's not the winning but the taking part", the fact remains that the big question is always "Yeah, but who won?". We can't help ourselves – we want to know who's best (especially if it's us...).

It was along such noble principles that the switch from matchplay to strokeplay was made in 1759 at St Andrews. In previous years the club champion, or holder of the Silver Club, had been decided by matchplay results i.e. competitors won matches by winning more holes than their opponent. The player who won by the most holes was champion. Of course, this meant that an erratic golfer could still win matches with low scores on some holes despite racking up cricket scores on others.

After several players pointed this out (presumably with observations along the lines of: "But it's not fair – I'm miles better than him."), the club agreed to switch to strokeplay – whereby the champion was the player who went around the whole course in the least strokes.

Golfers had no reason to complain ever again...

10 Heavyweight golf

Willie Park and Tom Morris battle for the belt

Although you normally associate belts with boxing, you could equally associate them with golf. If you wanted. Which would actually be quite appropriate if you lived in 1860 and played in the Prestwick "Open". Which you don't and you didn't. But never mind. Willie Park did. And so did Tom Morris. And over the next few years they had quite a battle for the Prestwick challenge belt: a red Moroccan strip of leather adorned with silver plates and worth some 30 guineas.

The tournament began in 1860 and was soon open to the great and the good of the day, but it was Park and Morris who proved the heavyweights, constantly swapping first and second place between each other and winning the event three times each in the first seven years.

Nowadays the tournament is better known as The Open (or British Open). You no longer win the leather, but no-one seems to mind. Belting!

11 Women! Playing golf!

Disreputable damsels get in on the act

Oh my! Just as golf was growing into the reputable sport we've come to know and love, who had to come along and disreputabilise its reputability? Women, that's who!

Yes, those devils in skirts infiltrated the game early on. Musselburgh and Wimbledon were the first culprits, founding women's clubs back in 1872. The Musselburgh fish ladies (as they were known) used to have a Shrove Tuesday match in which the "marrieds" apparently always beat the "unmarrieds".

St Andrews, Carnoustie and Pau in France soon also allowed women to compete. Although, as Miss A. M. Steward commented at the time in *The Gentlewomen's Book of Sports*: "A damsel with even one putter in her hand was labelled a fast and almost disreputable person." Well, quite...

12 The Claret Jug

Morris and son dominate the Open

You may remember Tom Morris. (Well you should – he cropped up in moments seven and ten of this illustrious tome). However, his son Tom Morris Jr is also well worth a mention. Like his father Old Tom, Young Tom won The Open belt three time. But as he did it three times in a row, he was allowed to keep the belt – which was subsequently replaced the following year by the famous Claret Jug. Young Tom won that too.

He also made the record books for scoring the first hole in one at The Open and for being the youngest winner of the tournament (aged 17). He and his dad frequently found themselves vying for the top of the leaderboard at tournaments. Although Tom Morris Sr could presumably always get the edge by sending the young whippersnapper to his room without his tea…

13 Boffins take shine to golfe

Oxford and Cambridge universities embrace the game

Back in the days when Britain still had an empire and the land was still "blessed" with a class system, approval from the establishment was considered a good, nay, an important thing.

Many olden-day golfers were no doubt thrilled, therefore, when their favourite sport received ringing endorsments from those most established of all establishments, Oxford and Cambridge Universities.

Cambridge, who had previously been quite instrumental in the development of football, were first to found a University Golf Club in 1875. But the same year Oxford followed suit. The two universities were soon battling it out in inter-collegiate, um, battles, while non-boffins carried on enjoying the game they had already been enjoying before the gowns and mortar board crews got involved. Which may mean endorsment from the universities was, in fact (cough), somewhat academic.

14 Tie trouble

Bob Martin's contentious Open victory

Controversy, eh? All sports experience the joys of a dispute at some point and golf is no exception. The first major "incident" in the game's fledgling history came at the second Open to be contested at St Andrews, in 1876. Bob Martin, a St Andrews member, finished the tournament with a total of 176. The only player within reach of his score was non-St Andrews member David Straith.

Straith's final round was somewhat disrupted when, at the 15th hole, a shot of his hit another player, playing out on an outward hole. The player (an upholsterer by trade, trivia fans) was relatively unscathed, but Straith was shaken by the incident. He dropped a shot, and another at the 16th, then hit a five and a six to finish the tournament tied with Martin. However, it was then declared that his approach shot at the 17th had arrived before the players in front had cleared the green. There was no evidence that this had improved the position of his ball, but a protest was lodged.

Straith insisted the protest should be resolved before a play-off. There was no referee appointed to adjudicate such matters and, in the ensuing melee, Martin was awarded victory because of the fact that he turned up for said play-off whereas Straith didn't.

All in all, it was a rather knotty situation (sorry).

15 Double hat-trick!

Anderson and Ferguson's triple triumphs

Hat-tricks, eh? Oh, sorry, did we start the last one like that? Still, you wait all day for one then two come along at once. Well, within a few years of each other anyway.

First to the magical trio was Jamie Anderson, who won The Open in 1877, 1878 and 1879 at Musselburgh, Prestwick and St Andrews respectively.

Almost usurping Anderson was Bob Ferguson, who won The Open in 1880, 1881 and 1882. He nearly made it four in a row but was narrowly pipped in 1883 by Willie Fernie, who sunk a lengthy putt at the 36th hole of their two-man play-off for victory. Ferguson liked it, but not a lot. Um, probably.

16 The train takes the strain

Lytham and St Anne's encourages commuters

Location, location, location. It's very important. Especially if you lived in the 19th century and were trying to establish a golf course. Fortunately for Alexander Doleman, his suggestion of locating a course near a railway proved particularly effective.

Having tried unsuccessfully to persuade the good folk of Blackpool to set up 18 holes for his pleasure, Doleman moved south and began campaigning at St Anne's. His theory was that by building a course near

the station, people could commute there with ease. St Anne's Hotel became the clubhouse and visitors could step off the train and cross the road for a quick round. Conveniently, the railway agreed to ring a bell when a train was pulling in, so golfers finishing their drinks at the 19th could pick up their hats and coats and saunter back in time to get the train home.

Blackpool, meanwhile, had to make do with having a pier.

17 Amateur dramatics

Disputes over who was being paid and who wasn't

When is an amateur not an amateur? When someone pays him, of course. Er, unless it isn't very much. Or before their 16th birthday. Confused? Yes, well so were the golfing authorities who hadn't quite got to grips with the tricky business of money in the early days.

For example, Douglas Rolland was ruled out of amateur play after accepting prize money for finishing second in the 1884 Open. However, the ten shillings that were paid to John Ball for a high finish were okay because he wasn't yet 16. And anyway, he probably blew the cash on trainers and alcopops.

Even so, the amateur/pro debate was a Branston of a pickle that would continue to marinate for some years to come.

"Are you sure you're an amateur...?"

18 On the Ball

The motorcycling gardener who enjoyed a spot of golf

Actually, thinking about it, John Ball (Remember him? We mentioned him five seconds ago on the last page…) probably didn't spend his winnings on alcopops. Partly because they didn't exist in the late 19th century, but predominantly because he had so many other interests. Despite his prodigious golfing talents, he was quite happy to be away from the course. Motorcycling and gardening were a couple of his passions (although, presumably, not at the same time...).

When he could tear himself away from his zinnias, he did enjoy winning. And frequently. As well as the 1890 Open – making him the first Englishman to break the Scottish pros' domination of the event – he could count eight amateur championships amongst his tally. Vroom!

19 Dead man golfing

Woking's spooky golf course

Makers of scary movies have a couple of locations that always seem to have the desired creepy effect. For example, that old house on the hill with the creaky door and the constant lightning storm. Or the graveyard that seems to be in perpetual fog. Or Woking Golf Club. What's that? Oh, okay, there haven't been an awful lot of films set there, but put it this way, we wouldn't fancy a midnight stroll across the fairways there.

In 1892, the club acquired its land from one Necropolis Company. Necropolis (meaning "City of the Dead") had plenty of land available – they had got it cheap to build cemeteries on. Some decades later, when cheap suburban train fares gave Woking a thriving (and living) populace, it was sold on to the golf club. To this day, players approaching the 18th tell of a spectre screaming from the bunkers. Unless of course we just made that last bit up. Boo!

20 Golfe goes global!

Jocks export ye olde sport to the world

It's fair to say some Scottish exports have succeeded better than others. Sean Connery and whisky – yes. Kilts and "soulsters" Wet Wet Wet – um, not so much.

Golf, however, has become a global success. Whether or not the game was actually invented in Scotland (see our thorough investigation on page eight), it certainly gained popularity there first. But it wasn't long before the rest of the world started to catch up.

England, France, India and Canada were early converts. And by the end of the 19th century the United States were also on board. Soon, vacation golf venues were being developed in Virginia, Florida and California. All of which somewhat undermined the American commentator who, in 1892, observed that: "Golf will never grip America like that other Scotch game, curling."

Well, we suppose that he was half right...

21 Bounding Billy

Rubber-cored ball invented

Science is a wondrous thing. It can put a man on the moon, grow crops without rain and, best of all, make a golf ball go further than ever before!

In 1898, patent rights were granted to Coburn, Haskell and Bertram on their invention of a rubber-cored golf ball.

This seemingly innocuous fact was to have a profound effect on the game. The new ball left the club face quicker, bounced harder and travelled faster. In fact, some said it bounced too hard and was "uncontrollable", earning it the nickname Bounding Billy (we get the bounding bit, but are not sure where the Billy came from...)

The cynicism diminished somewhat (like, completely) when Walter Travis won the US Amateur Championship with "Billy" in 1901 and the following year's US and British Open winners were also converts.

Soon, everyone was using it. And the scientific community partied like it was 1899. Which it had been. Quite recently.

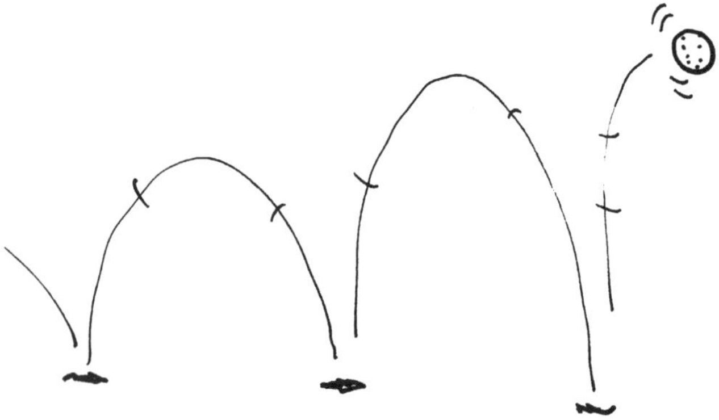

22 Not so bounding birdie

Unlucky flier helps invent golf term

A bird in the hand may be worth two in the bush, but a bird on the ground is worth one off the par. (Do you see what we've done there – clever, eh? Alright... please yourself.) Or rather it was for George Crump who, while playing in Atlantic City, lofted a wayward shot that smacked into a passing bird. The bird was felled, but the ball landed within inches of the hole. A delighted George putted for a better-than-expected score and thus the term "birdie" was invented.

We're not sure what happened to the inspirational bird, but we suspect its feathers were a little ruffled by the whole incident.

23 Wiggle while you work

The wisdom of the waggle

At its most Zen-like, golf is all in the mind. *Will* the ball where you want it to go. Pause. Then, pause a little more. Get your head in just the right place as you address the ball, let your body be a conduit for your mind. Ready? Ah, now feel the power of your own thoughts as you strike the ball… perfect!

Alternatively, you could just waggle your club and wiggle your backside. That's what 1902 Open winner Alexander "Sandy" Herd did and it worked for him. Before shots, he would waggle and wiggle to loosen any tension. Soon, others were imitating his move and golf became full of wagglers and wigglers. Which, in its own way, is a beautiful thing.

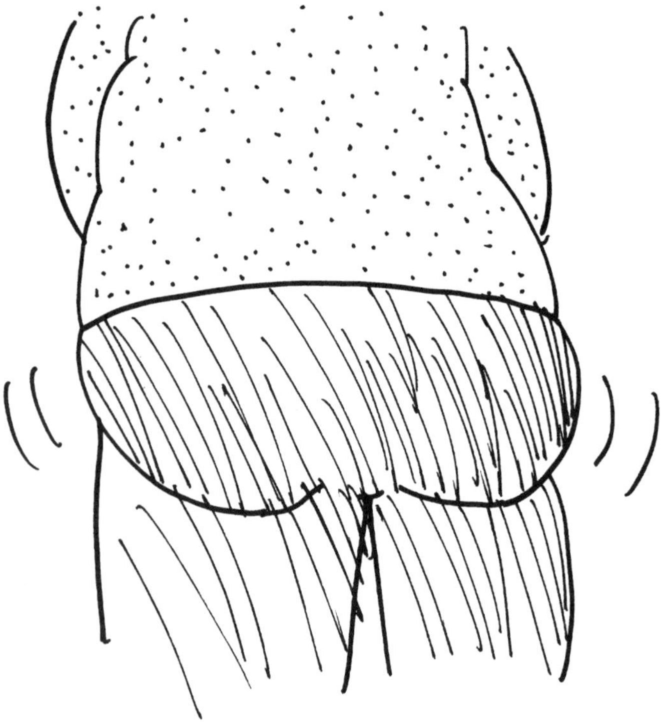

24 Breaking three hundred

Jack White smashes the British Open record

Like the first climber atop Everest, the first explorer to reach the North Pole or the first pilot to break the sound barrier, Jack White walked a similar path of previously untrodden ground when he won the 1904 British Open.

His achievement? Well, other than winning the bloomin' tournament, he was the first player in Open history to complete all four rounds in under 300. And that was after hitting a first-round 80. Subsequent rounds of 75, 72 and 69 game him a final tally of 296.

The 300 had crumbled and would never be such an imposing figure again.

25 Vive le difference!

Massey gains a trophy and a daughter in the same week

There are all sorts of reasons why we have the names we do. Perhaps you were named after your grandma, or a rich uncle or the city where you were conceived. None of which are a problem if those things are, say, Sarah, Tom or Paris. But if your Dad was Arnaud Massey and, in 1907, he'd just become the first Frenchman to win the British Open, you may have had room for concern (well, if a baby has concerns other than breast milk and crying).

After a final round of 77 to secure victory by two strokes, the delighted Monsieur Massey dashed to see his newborn baby daughter in hospital. Still on a high from his win, he promptly decided to name her after the links where he'd secured the trophy.

The result? Hoylake Massey. *Voilà*!

"Thank goodness you didn't win at Ballybunion..."

26 Little fella wins US Open

Wee Fred McLeod's big victory

Size isn't everything. How many times have you read a tale that began like that? Well, add one more to that number!

Size isn't everything and, in 1908, Fred McLeod massively proved the point. The diminutive golfer from the Midlothian Club weighed a tiny 108 pounds when he came over to the big ol' US of A in 1903, but soon began to rack up some humungous performances.

Like the puny jockeys he largely resembled, McLeod rode his luck big time to reach a little play-off with Willie Smith after both players had finished the US Open with not-particularly-small scores of 322.

But a 77 in the head-to-head gave McLeod a ginormous six-stroke margin of victory. It was an immense day for little Fred who presumably larged it afterwards.

27 Suffragettes on the rampage

Women protestors hit the greens. With stones

The early 20th century was a turbulent time. Especially for women, who were somewhat miffed at being treated like second-class citizens. Hence the rise of the suffragette movement, led by Emmeline Pankhurst.

Ms Pankhurst and friends decided to go on a campaign of window-smashing and thought they'd get some stone-throwing practice in first at Woking golf course.

When Emmeline's first throw almost hit a friend's dog, it was clear that practice was a good idea, but club members, never the most enlightened folk, were in no rush to admit suffragettes to the course again, lest they chained themselves to the flags to prepare for a Downing Street protest or something.

28 Amateur championed

Francis Ouimet wins the US Open

The American press had always favoured the amateur game over the professional. Mostly because it was played by well-heeled folk from high society, and, in those days, papers liked posh people. In 1913, however, they found an amateur they could champion and whom their readers could actually relate to.

Francis De Sales Ouimet (okay, he sounds posh too, but he wasn't) used to work as a caddie at the Country Club, Brookline, but having qualified for the US Open there, he proceeded to take the legends of the day – Johnny McDermott and Harry Vardon – all the way to a play-off.

He was accompanied by Eddie Lowery, his ten-year-old caddie. Many predicted Lowery was too young to be of any use, but he proved a canny advisor. Ouimet went on to win the play-off and the trophy and was promptly declared "World's Golf Champion" by the *New York Times*. Soon, posh people were very unpopular indeed.

"I don't mind an amateur winning…I just wish his name was shorter."

29 The long and short of it

James Braid gets "longer"!

Ever woken up and felt oddly different? No, being hungover doesn't count. Well, that's what happened to James Braid. No, not that he was hungover (will you get off that!). He genuinely was different. His drives suddenly went much further than they had before. It was very Mulder-and-Scully-like in its spookiness.

Braid himself admitted: "It was as though I went to bed a short driver and got up in the morning a long driver. It was then, and is still, the greatest golfing mystery I have ever come across."

However it happened though, the results were unmistakable: Braid started dominating the game, winning the British Open five times during the first decade of the 20th century, and he continued to play to a spectacularly high standard right into his 70s.

Was he in fact an alien? There is absolutely no evidence to support that theory. So we reckon, yes.

"Ooh, his balls go miles these days."

30 The Vardon grip

How Harry's hands took a hold on the game...

James Braid, J.H. Taylor and Harry Vardon became known as The Great Triumverate as between them, they dominated the pre-war game. Taylor, like Braid won the British Open five times while Vardon went one better and won it six times. But while all three could claim to have had a hold on the game, only one, quite literally, had a grip on it.

Harry Vardon's technique for gripping the club unsurprisingly became known as the Vardon Grip and is still used by most players today. For the right-handed golfer, it involved the little finger of the right hand overlapping the index finger of the left in, to use Vardon's words, "a marriage".

But while today's players still show no sign of, ahem, divorcing themselves from the Vardon Grip, it's actually unlikely that Harry invented it. The grip had already been used by at least one other player before Vardon (the Scottish amateur Johnny Laidlay) and J.H. Taylor also used it. But Harry became more famous than either of those two and the name stuck. Gripping stuff, eh?

31 Pro sport

USPGA is formed to give game a more sober image

American golfers didn't always have the best of reputations. Unlike today's squeaky-clean heroes, such as John Daly, the golfer of yore was often considered, in the parlance of the day, to be somewhat footloose, possibly inebriate, and certainly not a gentleman. How this reputation was earned is unclear, although we're happy to speculate wildly that it was all to do with lots of spoilt, rich playboys larking around while the rest of us decent folk tried to earn a crust.

Anyway, 15 years after the Brits had set up a professional body – the British Professional Golfers Association – America decided to follow suit, hoping to improve public perception of the sport. The USPGA was thus formed in 1916 and all top American golfers raised a hip flask to a more respectable future.

"I'm a professhhional, don't you know..."

32 The tee is invented!

Dentist makes all the difference

Sometimes it's the little things that make the difference. Like the tee. How did we survive before its existence? Well, actually, by piling up some sand or earth. But who wants to do that? It makes your hands all dirty! Fortunately, thanks to a New Jersey dentist called William Lowell, we don't have to. In 1920, when not pulling out teeth with pliers (which he might have done), "Butcher Bill" (which he might have been nicknamed) invented the tee. It was his idea to make a wooden peg with a round, concave top and a point at the bottom. He called it the "Reddy Tee". It caught on, and the world was a better place. But we still don't like going to the dentist.

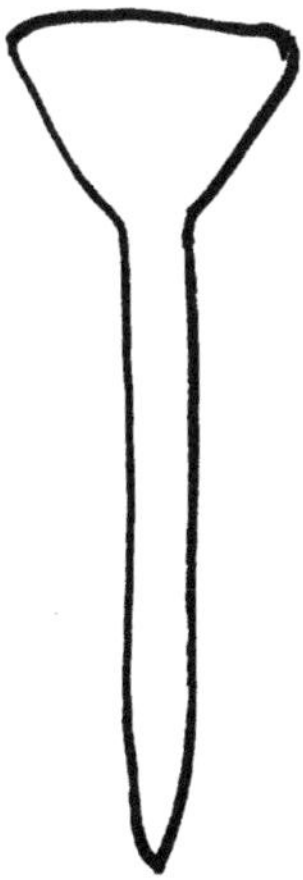

33 Big hands, big feet and no brains

"Sir" Walter Hagen's theories on golf, life and women...

Look out, the Americans are coming! That was the cry in the early 1920s. Well, maybe not the cry but... well, anyway, they were coming. The 1922 British Open was evidence of that. Three of the top four places were filled by US players. And following swiftly on from America's defeat of Great Britain and Ireland in the inaugural Walker Cup, it was proof enough that the States were now a golfing nation to be reckoned with.

At the forefront of this charge was the 1922 Open victor, Walter Hagen, *aka* "Sir Walter", *aka* "The Haig". When not acquiring nicknames, Walter would normally be pursuing one of his many other interests. These included collecting trophies (he won The Open four times, the US Open twice and the USPGA five times); exhibition games (no-one did more to popularise the game in the US); good food and wine (he'd often arrive at matches with luxurious hampers of the stuff) and women ("Call them all 'Sugar' and you won't go too far wrong").

Walter liked good living and the lucrative exhibtion match circuit gave him the means to live how he liked. "I never wanted to be a millionaire," he said, "I just wanted to live like one." And he did, on occasion driving from courses in an open Rolls-Royce bouncing balls into the crowd.

Despite the fact that he was

clearly very good at golf, he never gave the impression of taking it too seriously, once commenting: "Give me a man with big hands, big feet and no brains and I will make a golfer out of him."

Although our favourite Hagen quote remains the simple: "Never hurry, never worry and don't forget to smell the roses on the way."

Whether the roses squirted water at anyone who got too close, we couldn't say...

34 Darwin puts theory into practice

Legendary golf reporter Bernard Darwin turns player in hour of need

Times SPORT

Darwin to the rescue!

By Bernard Darwin

Your reporter has seen some magnificent golf in his time. But rarely have I been so transfixed by a player's talent as I was at the first official Walker Cup match between the United States and Great Britain. Who was the player who so transfixed me with his transfixing skills? Why, it was me! Yes, Bernard Darwin. *Times* reporter extraordinaire. Naturally, I don't want to overstate my part in events but it's fair to say I was magnificent.

It all began when Britain's captain Robert Harris fell ill on the eve of the tournament. Who could take his place at such short notice? If only there was a British journalist covering the tournament who was also a useful golfer...

There was. It was me. I stepped in. It all worked out. End of story.

Um, except to say that Britain lost 8-4. Although it wasn't my fault. I won my match. Even though I was hit on the chest by a ball during practice!

Anyway, the tournament was a great success and went on to be a fixture of the golfing calendar.

As a little footnote, it's worth pointing out that I was also brilliant in the post-match press conference. Where my wit and charm enthralled the assembled media - in particular the reporter from The *Times* who wrote this story. Who was me.

35 It's great when you're straight!

Joyce Wethered's amazing accuracy

The phrase' "You hit like a girl" has rarely been used as a compliment, but if the "girl" in question was Joyce Wethered then it would be. Er, if the person saying it had heard of Joyce, that is.

Who she?

Joyce Wethered was possibly the straightest hitter in the history of the game, male or female. She first came to major prominence when she won the English Women's Amateur championship at the tender age of 19, the first of five consecutive wins. She also won the British Womens' championship four times (1922, 1924, 1925 and 1929).

The legendary Bobby Jones once said: "I have not played golf with anyone, man or woman, who made me feel so utterly outclassed."

The secret of her success was her immaculate swing and an unerring ability to hit the ball so straight that Scottish pro Willie Wilson was once moved to observe: "My god, mon! She could hit a ball 240 yards on the fly while standing barefoot on a cake of ice." Although, as far as we know, Joyce never actually hit a ball from an iced cake.

"Oh, Joyce has been practising again..."

36 Bada Bing!

Crooner's decent golfing record

At the age of 22, Bing Crosby, a golf fanatic and former caddie, won the 1922 United States Musicians' Golf Championship. It was just one event in the singer's lifetime love affair with the sport. He competed in both the American and British Amateur championships and set up the "Clambake", as the Bing Crosby Pro-Am was known. He is also one of the only people to score a hole-in-one at Cypress Point, Florida.

Our copious research reveals that, between rounds, Bing also managed to squeeze in a few albums and films.

THE CUT

37 To putt is human...

... to diegel is divine!

dieffenbachia /di:f(e)n'bakia/ *n* any plant of the tropical American evergreen perennial genus *Dieffenbachia,* some species of which are grown as pot plants for their handsome variegated foliage. The plants are poisonous and the sap is extremely acrid: family *Acraceae.* [named after Ernst *Dieffenbach* (died 1855), German horticultuist]

Diégo-Suarez (*French* djegoshares) *n* the former name of **Antseranana**

diegel /dai'gull/ v. (*to diegel*) a term first coined during the inaugural Ryder Cup. **1** In 1927 the USA beat Great Britain somewhat convincingly with nine wins and a half in twelve matches. **2** One of the members of the US team was Leo Diegel. **3** Diegel's putting technique was, well, quite mad. **4** Having had many putting woes over the years, he had adopted a unique method on the greens. **5** He would crouch, with his chin close to the top of the grip, elbows stuck out either side and feet far apart. **6** This method proved so successful for him that other players started to adopt it. **7** This led to reporter Bernard Darwin (remember him?) coining the verb 'to diegel' – I diegel, thou dieglest, he diegels, we all diegel! **8** Which gave us the idea to arrange this story in the form of a dictionary definition (see 'lame' for further reference)

die-hard *or* **diehard** *n* **1** a personwho resists change or who holds onto an untenable position or outdated attitude. **2** (*modifier*) obstinately resistant to change. **'die- hardism** *n*

38 Walter calls a cab

The Haig loses trophy... quite literally!

After a run of 22 unbeaten USPGA tournament matches, Walter "The Haig" Hagen's unstoppable progress was finally, um, stopped in 1928 by Leo "The Dictionary" Diegel (okay, nobody ever called him that…) at the Baltimore Country Club.

It was a relief as much as anything for Diegel to win because he'd previously suffered numerous embarrasing defeats at the hands of Hagen, often when he had what should have been unassailable leads.

However, it would be a while before Diegel could savour the USPGA trophy. Asked where it was, Hagen replied: "I can't remember. I might have left it in a cab…"

39 Jones does Grand Slam...

... with his trusty putter "Calamity Jane"

Teen prodigy Bobby Jones began trying to win major golf titles aged 14, and after a series of near misses, he claimed his first US Open title seven years later in 1923.

Jones wielded a rusty old putter that he called "Calamity Jane", but the only calamity was for anyone who had the misfortune of playing against him once he got it. In 1930, he achieved the "Impregnable Quauadrilateral", winning the British Open, British Amateur, US Amateur and US Open, a feat never achieved before or since. With 13 majors to his credit, Jones retired from serious competition, aged 28, and went on to build the beautiful Augusta National golf course and invent The Masters. Yee-haw!

40 Up, up and away!

Balloon ball deflates top stars

It's not always the case that a change is as good as a rest. Sometimes a change is arrest. Um, sort of. That is to say, players felt trapped… nay, imprisoned, when the USPGA insisted that, in 1931, they all start using the new "balloon ball" in competition. This wasn't actually a balloon, mind. Just a slightly lighter ball. It was supposed to ensure players couldn't hit it too far, and also that it would sit better in the coarser grass common to American courses. However, the pros complained that it had a tendency to "get away" when played in windy conditions. After two years, the authorities agreed and the players were released from their obligation to use the new ball. You could say (and we will) that the bubble (alright, balloon) had well and truly burst.

41 Gene genius

Sand wedge ploy and Sandwich joy for Sarazen!

Depression? What depression? Despite the fact that, in 1932, most of America was still suffering from the Great Depression, it was a boom year for Gene Sarazen.

Although he too had lost a bundle of money in the stock market crash, Sarazen picked himself up and soared again – quite literally!

A mate of aviator-turned-recluse Howard Hughes, Sarazen was having flying lessons when a pull on the joystick and the plane's immediate climb inspired him to alter his niblick (the equivalent of today's nine iron). Thus, the sand wedge was born.

Sarazen tested his new club at the British Open played at Prince's in Sandwich, Kent. Untroubled by Prince's big bunkers, he set a record score of 283 and won The Open by five shots. Fifteen days later, he won the US Open at Fresh Meadow. He was flying!

42 Dr Stableford's system

The doc who helped duffers compete with experts

It's an age old problem. You want to play a game of something but the only person available to compete with (mum, boyfriend, the cat...) isn't as good as you, thereby taking all the sport out of it. So, what do you do? Fortunately for golf, Dr Frank Stableford had the perfect, er, prescription.

He devised a system, first used at Wallasey near Liverpool, that awarded points for performance against par, with an allowance for handicaps. Suddenly you could play any old duffer and still make a game of it. Hooray!

So give your mum a call and get out on the course (don't bother with the cat – they never fill in their cards properly...).

"It's a great system, doc, but I can't read your writing."

43 Cotton buds

We, er, wax lyrical over Henry's Open triumphs...

By 1934, the British Open had been dominated by American winners for a whole decade, but Henry Cotton, from Cheshire, put a stop to all that (well, for a little while at least...).

During qualifying, he hit a 66 and then proved it was no fluke by scoring 67 in the first round at Sandwich. Then, to prove that that wasn't a fluke either, he hit a record 65 on the second day (the popular Dunlop 65 ball was named after that). Even a dodgy stomach and a 79 in the final round couldn't stop him winning The Open.

He repeated the feat twice more (winning The Open, that is, not having gut aches) and revitalised British golf in the process.

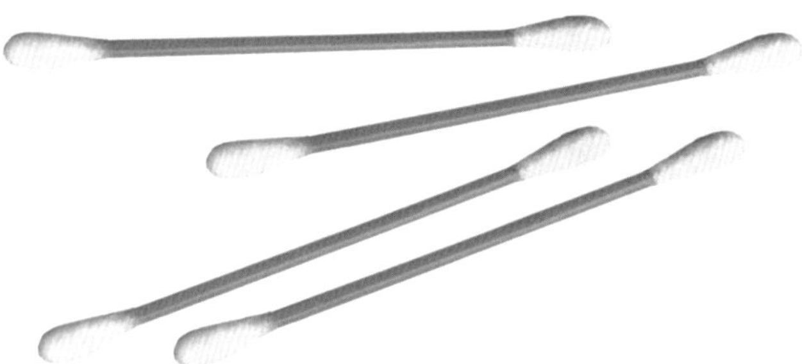

44 Patty goes wild

Forrrrrrrrre!

Exhibition games are supposed to be an exhibition of great golf, hence the name. However, in 1938, US Womens' Amateur champion Patty Berg took the novel approach of making a total exhibition of herself instead.

The normally pretty useful Berg somehow managed to hit five people with her wild shots in the first nine holes of an exhibition match with Walter Hagen.

Even The Haig's famous fondness for the fillies took a knock: "I don't know about that girl – she's dangerous," he exclaimed before presumably diving for safety behind his Rolls-Royce.

Sadly, the exciting concept of "Hit the spectator" never really took off as a competitive sport.

45 It's war!

Risk of imminent death inspires rule amendment

Who says the golfing authorities are behind the times? In a prompt reaction to the fact that World War Two was going on all around them, the powers that be made a subtle addition to the rules of play. In brief, the amended rules stated that during gunfire or while bombs were falling, players could take cover without penalty for ceasing play. It was a thoughtful decision that made the whole ghastly six years much more bearable.

Elsewhere, the war was having other effects on the game. Financially, it was a disastrous time for clubs' courses – many courses didn't see a mower for years and the grass was kept down by grazing sheep and cattle. Trenches were dug across fairways to hinder landings by hostile aircraft, while Wentworth concealed a key command post all through the war. It was definitely not a "boom" time for golf.

46 Jimmy in tune

Former nightclub singer wins The Masters

Presumably, quite a few nightclub singers play a little golf in their spare time. But we doubt many professional golfers do a little nightclub singing in their off hours.

Except Jimmy Demaret. (See, you knew we were going somewhere with this…) Demaret had been a late-night crooner before taking up golf professionally. It proved the right decision. In 1940, he won The Masters by a record four strokes.

Off the course, his trademark was the high-heeled Texas boots he always wore. He also continued to entertain, often in the company of Bing Crosby. Although there's no evidence that he only sang when he was winning…

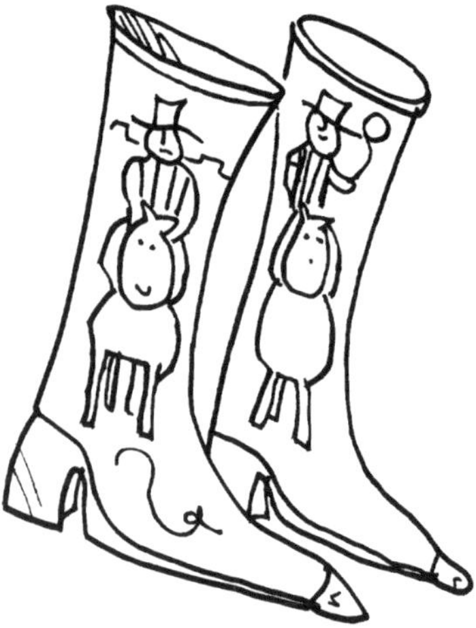

47 The Gold Dust Twins

Nelson and McSpadden clean up

WAR BOND

During the war, tournament winners were often paid in war bonds. And more often than not the winners were the "Gold Dust Twins" – Byron Nelson and "Jug" McSpadden.

What Nelson didn't win, McSpadden did, appeared to be the rule. In 1945, Nelson finished with $63,335.66 in war bonds. McSpadden wasn't too far behind.

Unfortunately for both, war bonds didn't keep their value particularly well after hostilities ended. Ironically, though, one item that really did was golf balls. Due to restrictions on production during the war, decent balls were at a premium and you could expect to pay around four dollars for a good pre-war ball in 1945.

And what is the moral of this story? Er, in times of war, it really pays to hang on to your balls.

48 Slammin' Sam Snead

Smooth swinger and wisecracker wins The Open

Looking like a cross between Bing Crosby and a prep schoolboy with his natty straw boater, "Slammin' Sam" Snead finally won his first national title when he captured the British Open in 1946.

Envied for his remarkbly smooth swing action and admired for his homespun charm ("Sometimes, when I putt, I look like a monkey trying to wrestle a football"), Snead was a popular figure – even when he didn't get the drinks in. "Sam was born with a natural ability to keep his bar bills as low as his golf scores," Jimmy Demaret once joked.

Later on, Snead would coach young players. His sage advice to one fairly hopeless student was: "Lay off for three weeks… then quit for good."

49 Muffin Face!

Bobby Locke eats up the US tour

Winning doesn't always make you popular. Take the case of Bobby Locke, for example. The six-times South African champion had once been a svelte young thing, but by the mid-1940s he was, not to put too fine a point on it, a bit of a porker. His features were what you would call "lived-in" and his gait was, ahem, stately. When he came on the US Tour after the war, critics christened him "Muffin Face".

However, what really annoyed American golfers wasn't Locke's cake head, but the fact that he was winning all their money. He arrived just in time for the 1947 Masters, where he finished a credible 14th, before going on to win four of the next five events. He then received $5,000 appearance money to compete in the Tam O'Shanter, which he won, before picking up the Canadian Open too, to finish the year second on the US Tour money list and with a whole a lot of dough in the bank.

50 Silent Ben

Deeds not words were Hogan's way

Although Walter "The Haig" Hagen was mighty popular with his chucklesome, larger-than-life antics and one-line zingers, his brashness didn't appeal to all Americans. Many wanted their idea of a hero – the strong but silent type; someone who thought more of deeds than words, and who achieved his success through hard work and sweat rather than inherent genius and spark. Sadly, Rambo hadn't yet been invented. And anyway, he didn't play golf (we think).

More usefully, in 1948, Ben Hogan won the British Open. "Silent Ben", as he was known, was exactly what America was looking for. He practised. A lot. He won tournaments. Loads of them. He spoke very little. Even after a near-death car crash, he steadily recovered and carried on winning. He won nine majors in total – four US Opens, two Masters and USPGA titles and one British Open – all won between 1948 and 1953. Shhh...

51 Turning Japanese

A post-war golf boom in the Orient

Ah, those ingenious Japanese. After the horrors of war, they spent the next few decades building up a thriving economy, westernising their culture and, most smartly, playing a lot more golf.

Their only problem was the lack of space to build enough golf courses to satisfy the huge demand… so they built multi-storey driving ranges, too! Ingenious, eh?

Now Japan has a thriving pro tour and a lot of amateurs bashing balls down the range. Jumbo Osaki!

52 Bradshaw bottles it

And the truth lies in broken shards...

Lies! They're brilliant! Well, some of them are. Usually, the ones that are funnier or more memorable than the truth. Such a lie grew up around Harry Bradshaw's attempt to win the 1949 British Open at Royal St George's.

Locked in a battle with, um, Bobby Locke, Bradshaw found himself having to take a shot at the sixth where his ball was surrounded by shards of glass from a broken bottle. Unwilling to risk hitting the ball, lest fragments might fly in his face, he took a dropped shot instead.

However, one sneaky newspaper claimed his ball had actually landed in a bottle, and set up a photo of a ball in a bottle to prove it.

The public much prefered this story and it stuck. Oh, and Locke won, in a play-off.

53 Babe's boobies!

Breasts hinder female athlete of the century

Pity poor ol' Babe Zaharias. Yes, she won Olympic golds in track and field events. Yes, she was an accomplished tennis and basketball player and probably the athlete of the century. And yes, in 1951, she did win seven of the LPGA's 16 events as part of a golfing career that saw her win every major women's golf event. However, think what she could have accomplished if she hadn't had boobies?!

As Babe herself acknowledged in her Texan drawl: "If ah didn't have these, ah'd hit the ball 20 yards further!"

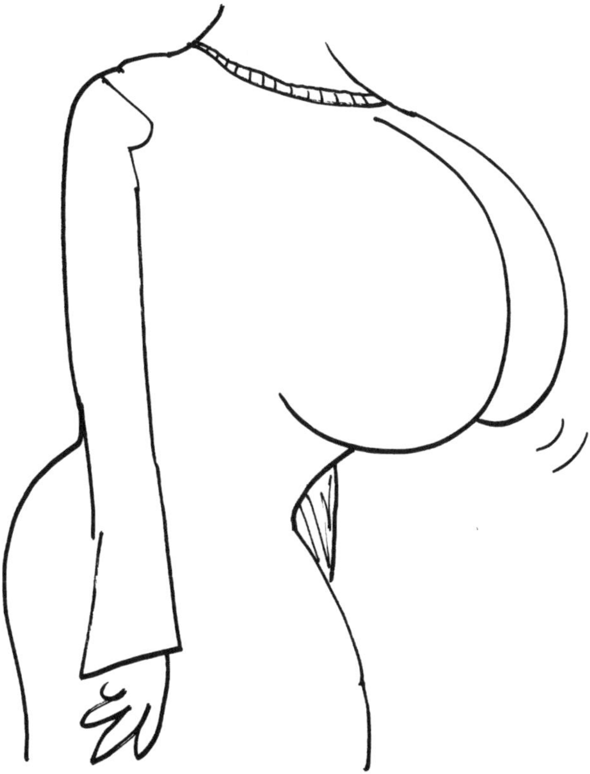

54 Confessions of a hooker

Bob Hope's life of golf

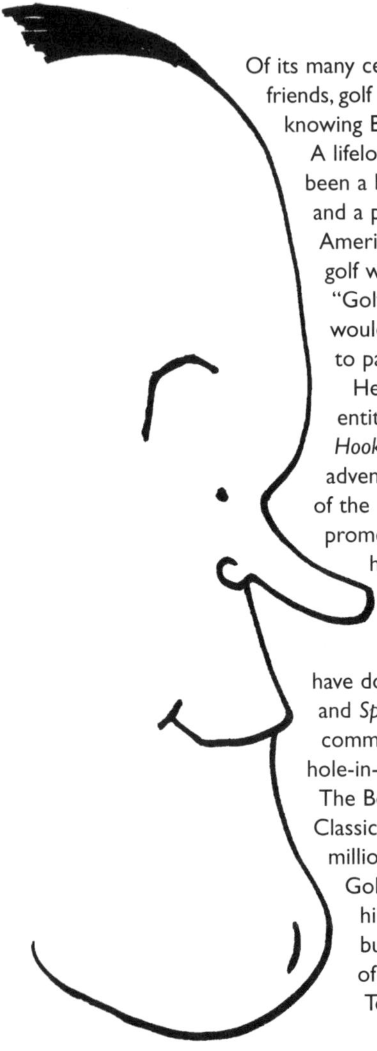

Of its many celebrated celebrity friends, golf has probably celebrated knowing Bob Hope the most.

A lifelong sports fan, Hope had been a boxer, a pool hustler and a part-owner of several American football teams, but golf was his game.

"Golf is my profession," he would say. "I only tell jokes to pay my green fees."

He wrote a bestseller entitled *Confessions of a Hooker* about his golfing adventures and spent much of the 1950s onwards promoting the game both at home and abroad.

The USPGA gave him a medal as "one of the three men who have done the most for golf" and *Sports Illustrated* commemorated his fifth hole-in-one with a silver cup. The Bob Hope/Chrysler Classic has raised over $40 million for charity and the Golf Hall of Fame declared him: "Not a golf champion but a great champion of golf".

Top hole!

55 Golfer in the White House

Ike swings into power

There here have been plenty of presidents, like celebrities, who enjoy a round, but only one true golfing nut has taken residence in the White House. President David Dwight Eisenhower (from now on let's call him "Ike") ran for office in 1951, with support from Bobby Jones, and had the USPGA construct a putting green in the White House garden.

Even Ike's official vacations were planned with golfing possibilities in mind. Of course, occasionally, pesky things like running the country got in the way of his golf time but, in 1958, his steady support of the game received worldwide recognition with the introduction of the The Eisenhower Trophy – 29 countries competed at St Andrews over four rounds of strokeplay in the first event. Unfortunately for the Prez, America were pipped in a play-off by Australia, whose foursome – Bruce Devlin, Robert Stevens, Doug Bachli and Peter Toogood – proved, er, too good for the Yanks.

56 Lew's screen shot

TV cameras capture final-hole drama

"Once upon a time," we'll tell our children, "there was no such thing as reality TV." Camera crews didn't follow hairdressers, bell boys, dinner ladies and drain inspectors around and make programmes about it. There used to be real telly full of drama and sport."

Naturally, they'll laugh and not believe us. And then they'll put us in a home.

But that time did exist. And not so long ago. The first nationally televised golf match in America was in 1953. Two million viewers tuned in to watch the "World Championship" at Tam O'Shanter and saw Lee Worsham's 135-yard wedge shot to the final green drop in the hole for a birdie, and a one-shot victory worth $25,000. It was a great advert for the game. As for adverts, nowadays – how bad have they got? Do you remember when… eh, what's that? Oh, apparently it's time for our nap.

57 Pung bung

You lose some, you earn some

Hawaiian golfer Jacqueline Pung thought she had won the US Women's Open in New York in 1957. After all, she had got the lowest score.

Unfortunately, her playing partner Betty Jameson, who was marking Pung's card, had made an error by writing a six instead of a five on one hole. Despite the fact that the total was correct, and Pung had "won", she was promptly disqualified.

Less unfortunately, the players had a whip-round and generously bunged Pung $3,000, some $1,200 more than the first prize!

58 The dentist

Open wide... it's another tooth-tampering golf story!

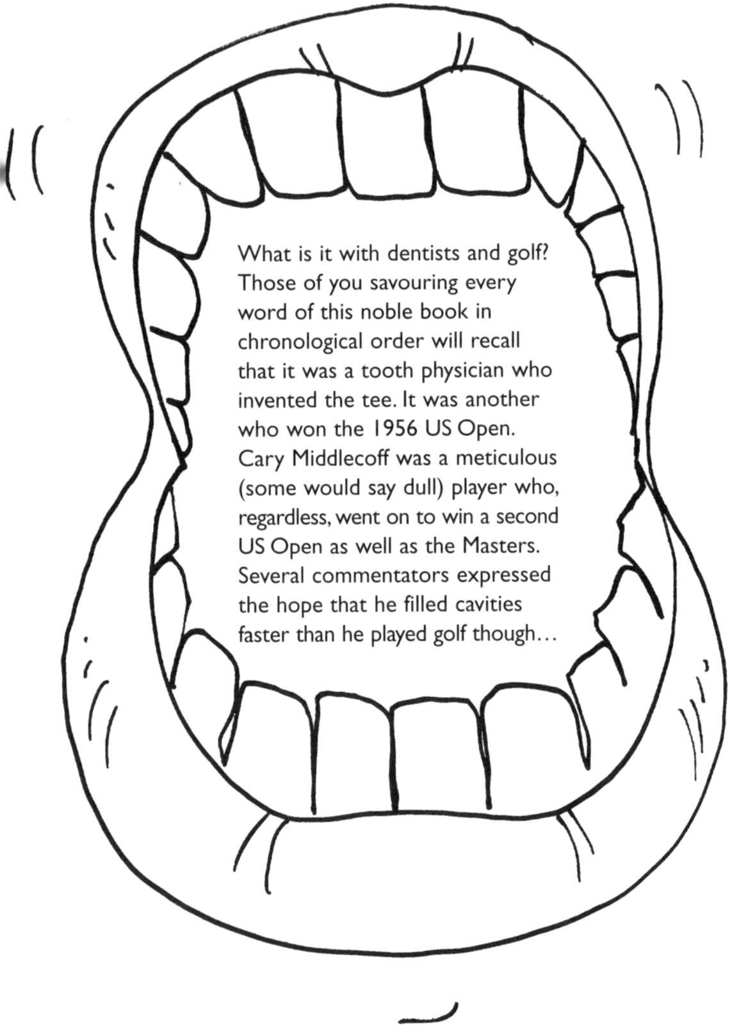

What is it with dentists and golf? Those of you savouring every word of this noble book in chronological order will recall that it was a tooth physician who invented the tee. It was another who won the 1956 US Open. Cary Middlecoff was a meticulous (some would say dull) player who, regardless, went on to win a second US Open as well as the Masters. Several commentators expressed the hope that he filled cavities faster than he played golf though…

59 Player's tears unfounded

Opponents snatch defeat from the jaws of victory

They say he who laughs last, laughs longest. Which doesn't really have any bearing on our tale as it's all about crying. In fact, a far more appropriate saying would be he who cries first, laughs longest. Er, sort of.

Anyway, the crier in question was Gary Player. Coming off the final green at the 1959 British Open at Muirfield, Player turned away in tears – having bunkered his drive and then three-putted, he knew he'd blown his chances of winning the tournament… except he hadn't, because no-one could take advantage of his mistakes.

One by one the leaders slipped away, unable to match his total of 284 and the previously blubbing 23-year-old cheered up significantly when he was crowned the youngest Open champion since Willie Auchterlonie in 1893. Six years later, he became only the third golfer to win all four modern majors with victory in the 65th US Open.

There, there...

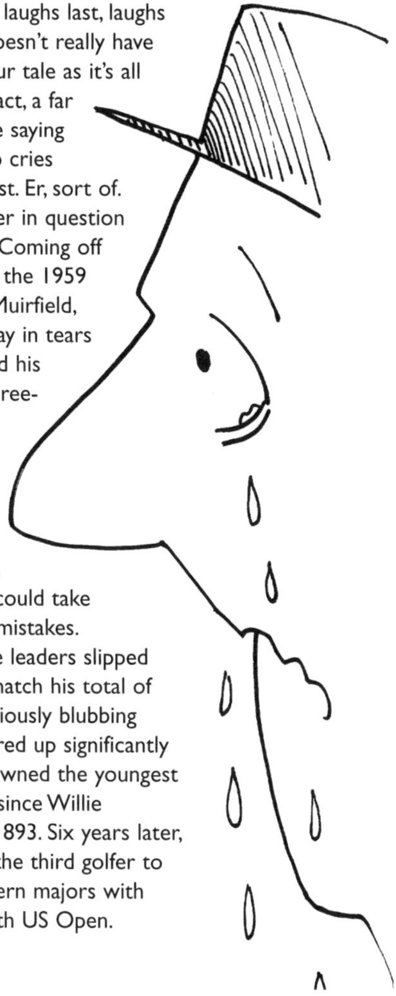

60 Dancer on the green

Showgirl Spearman wins Women's British Amateur title

Attractive young women have (rightly) always been wary of men who come up and say: "Has anyone ever told you that you could be a model." Well, that's certainly our experience anyway (suggesting they could be an actress, the prime minister or a shoe salesman haven't got us very far either…).

But when former showgirl Marley Spearman was approached in the golf department at Harrods, she heard a different proposition.

"Has anyone ever told you that you could be a golfer?" asked the shop's resident professional, having been impressed with her swing.

He was right to be impressed – she went on to win the Women's British Amateur title in 1961.

Rumours that she celebrated her victory by lining up a dozen opponents and proceeeded to do the can-can with them are, sadly, almost certainly fabricated for the sole purpose of providing this story with a punchline.

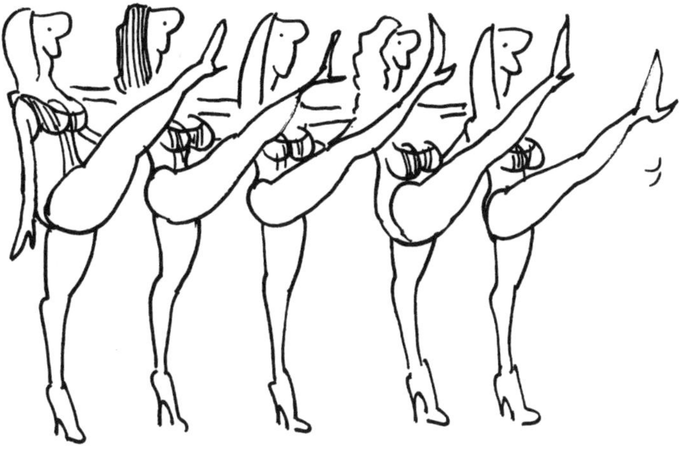

61 The Golden Bear emerges

Jack Nicklaus secures first professional win

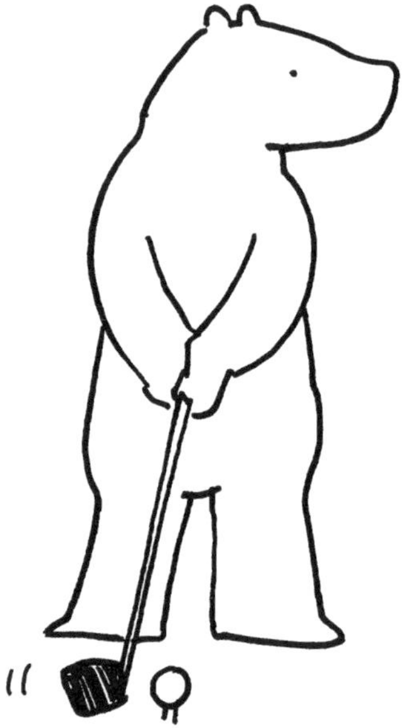

Any time a new young talent does well at sport, there is an immediate temptation for scurrilous writers, such as ourselves, to pronounce them the next big thing, then watch in disappointment as they fail to live up to their (our) promise. However, anyone making such predictions about the young Jack Nicklaus would have had years of smugness ahead.

Nicklaus had already won the Ohio Open at 16, the National Amateur twice and was only 22 when he went head-to-head with Arnold Palmer in the 1962 US Open. The tournament went to a play-off and the youngster, who was yet to gain his "Golden Bear" moniker, roared to victory with his superior putting. It would be the first of many victories (and the first of many opportunities for us to draw a bear).

62 Left, right...

You'll need a mirror to read this one!

Although there have been plenty of southpaws who have triumphed in tennis, for some reason there are practically none in golf. Or as Harry Vardon once rather more bluntly put it: "Left-handers? Never saw one who was worth a damn."

Clearly, he never saw Bob Charles play. In 1963, Charles became the first left-handed winner of a major, with his victory in the British Open.

Although other players, such as Ben Hogan, were born left-handed, they switched to right-handed clubs.

Oh, and just to add a little extra confusion (as if mirroring this text wasn't enough), Charles is actually right-handed. Except when he plays golf.

Clear? Great...

63 Venturi struggles to victory

Brave Ken toughs it out at the US Open

Golf can be tough sometimes, eh? You know, when you're a little off, not feeling your best. Maybe you didn't get a good night's sleep, or you think you might be coming down with something…

Our advice? Get over yourself! It's not like you're Ken Venturi.

Poor old Ken won the 1964 US Open but, by God, it was a struggle!

Okay, winning a major is never easy, but it was particularly tough for ol' Ken. For the previous two years, nerve damage restricted his left side and began to affect the circulation in his hands. He had barely qualified for the tournament. He was treated for heat prostration between rounds and had a doctor walking anxiously beside him for some of the tournament, but a wet towel around his neck and an 18-foot putt on the 15th green on the final day sustained him on the way to a memorable victory. Well, memorable for spectators – Venturi later admitted that he could recall little about the closing stages, such was his state.

So, remember plucky Ken's woes next time you feel like a moan!

"He's looking great to win the tournament…"

64

Big balls

Size does matter

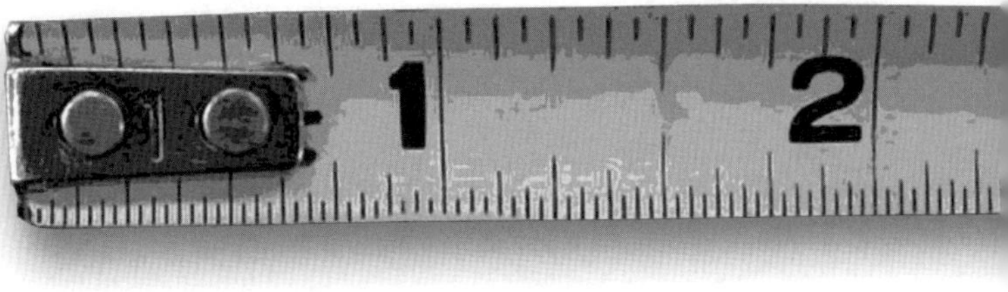

After a comprehensive defeat in the 1967 Ryder Cup (23-and-a-half to 8-and-a-half) some Brits felt that it was all a problem of balls – quite literally.

As the *Daily Telegraph*'s Leonard Crawley put it: "The Americans are superior because it takes more skill to play with 1.68 inch ball than it does with the traditional British 1.62 inch ball. It is much easier to go from the big to the little than from the little to the big."

Others agreed with him and, after some pondering, the authorities decided that, as with so many aspects of life, things could surely only be improved by having bigger balls. The following year, the larger ball was duly brought in on a three-year trial.

(Note: we'd like to apologise for the transparent glee we have displayed in writing a story all about big balls.)

65 US pros make new deal

TV money causes a row

It was the late '60s, man, and everyone was, er, high on life. Except US golfers. Who were low. The reason for their downer? All the extra money coming into the game from TV. It wasn't the money they objected to, but how the PGA weren't distributing it properly (i.e. into their pockets).

This led to a stand-off with players threatening to start their own organisation... hey, kinda like a protest movement! However, in 1968, the PGA gave in and a new division was set up within the organisation to represent players better. Power to the people!

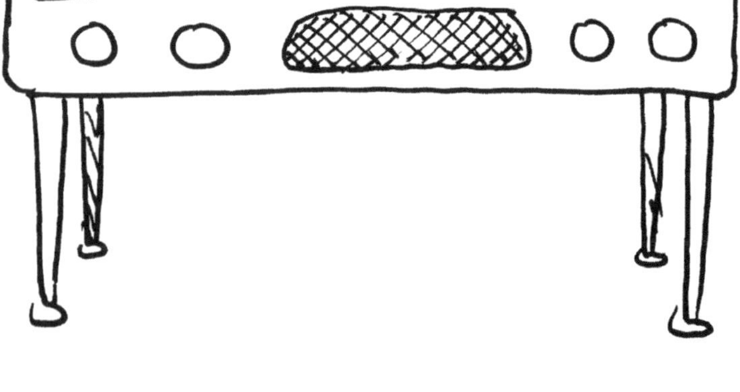

66 Who wants to be a millionaire?

Arnie pulls down a large wad of cash

A million dollars is a fair chunk of change now. In 1968 it was, well, loads more. But by the end of the year, that's how much Arnold Palmer had earned in career prize money – the first player to amass a million bucks.

One of the most charismatic golfers ever, Arnie was, and is, hugely popular (as well as being mega-successful and rich). His cavalier swing (he hit everything hard – even putts), combative style and expressive face made him an instant favourite with the crowds and the watching television audience. His fans became known as "Arnie's Army" and got to witness him win seven majors and a total of 60 PGA Tour wins.

He later moved on to the lucrative Seniors Tour where he has managed to earn a couple more million.

His bank manager must be a big fan, too. When not playing, Arnie has a string of successful business interests under the umbrella of Arnold Palmer Enterprises.

Safe to say, he's never short of a bob or two…

67 You betcha!

Sixties shooter Lee Trevino helps caddie win bet

Legend has it that Lee Trevino's caddie bet that his boss would score under 70 in every round of the 1968 US Open at Oak Hill. After three rounds of 69, 68 and 69, the bag carrier's wager was in good shape right up until the 72nd hole, where Trevino found himself in the rough. With shots in hand, rather than play safe, "Supermex" tried to blast his way onto the green. He didn't get out first time, but managed it second time before sinking his putt to finish with a 69. He thus won the tournament, equalled Jack Nicklaus' record aggregate of 275 and helped his caddie to a nice little bonus.

68 So close

The tightest Ryder Cup finish ever!

In 1969, the Ryder Cup was creating even more of a buzz than usual. The reason? Fans were salivating at the prospect of a potential face-off between the newly-crowned British Open champion, Tony Jacklin, and the greatest golfer of the age – but Ryder Cup rookie – Jack Nicklaus.

The match lived up to all the buzz and saliva with probably the most exciting finish ever seen. The match was poised at 15-and-a-half apiece as the two giants approached the final green in the last match. Nicklaus holed his putt from three feet and then picked up Jacklin's marker, which was eighteen inches from the cup, saying: "I am sure you would have holed but I wasn't prepared to see you miss."

The sporting gesture left the final score at 16-all: the Ryder Cup returned to America and the fans all calmed down a bit.

69 The voice of golf

Peter Alliss: the voice, the wisdom, the duffer

Sometimes the mic is mightier than the club. Er, or something.

In 1969, Peter Alliss retired from a professional playing career and moved into television commentary. Although a talented golfer and a regular Ryder Cup member during the 1950s and 1960s, he never really set the world on fire as a player (probably for the best – arson is a crime, kids).

However, as a commentator, he became world renowned with his work for the BBC in Europe and ABC in America.

The voice of golf, a beacon of wit and wisdom or a bit of an old duffer, depending on your point of view (although we would never suggest the latter), he can always be relied upon to offer a thought and a chuckle (often at the same time) during most tournaments on the box. He also had his own telly programme *A Round with Alliss*, has designed a few golf courses (including The Belfry) and written loads of books. But none, dear reader, as stupid or magnificent as this one, of course.

70 Gone with the wind

Jacklin blows away the competition

Like people, some golf courses just aren't very popular. It's not their fault, it just happens. Hazeltine National, venue of the 1970 US Open, was one such course. It was long, windy and difficult.

And, as we say, very unpopular. Particularly after the first round, where a combination of its large lake, many ponds, big dog legs guarded by enormous trees, and a howling wind ensured that nearly everyone struggled. Jack Nicklaus hit an 81, Gary Player an 80 and Arnold Palmer a 79. Dave Hill, who would go on to finish second, even went so far as to call the course designer, Robert Trent Jones, "an idiot".

However, one player who didn't dislike the course, or the conditions, was Tony Jacklin. The Brit managed an astonishing 71 on the first day and then held onto his lead for the next three rounds to claim victory. In doing so, Tony became the first British winner of the US Open since Ted Ray in 1920 and was blown away by his achievement.

71 Out of this world

Golf in space!

When astronaut Alan Shepard landed on the moon during the Apollo 14 mission of 1971, he spent hours trudging about in lunar dust, which was rather dull. Happily, he also brought along a collapsible golf club and two balls to play with and became the first person ever to hit golf shots on the moon. One-handed, too!

72 Snakes alive!

Prankster Lee commits daylight rubbery at the US Open

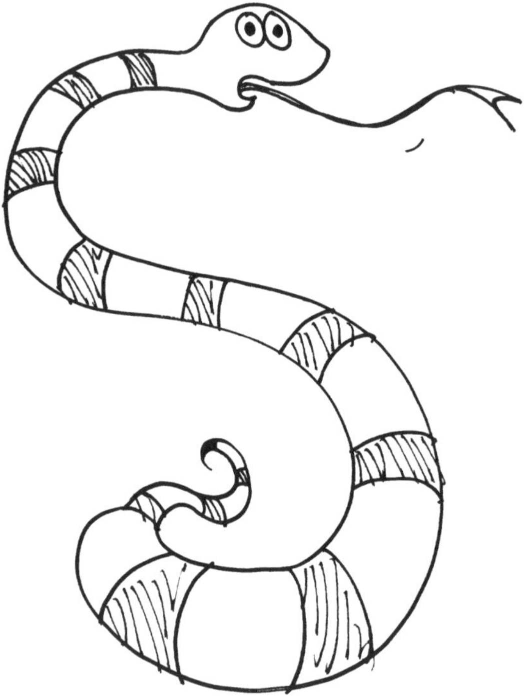

Lee Trevino enjoyed a great three-week spell in 1971 scoring successive victories in the US Open, the Canadian Open and the British Open. The British, he won by one stroke, the Canadian and US, both went to play-offs. An infamous prankster, Trevino began the US Open play-off by throwing a rubber snake at his opponent, Jack Nicklaus. Nicklaus might have considered it gamesmanship by anyone else, but as it was Trevino, he knew there was nothing snakey, sorry, sneaky about the gesture.

IT'S A PLAY-OFF!

73 Bunny golfer... not

Playboy develop a fleeting interest in golf...

Pretty 16-year-old Laura Baugh became the youngest winner of the US Women's Amateur championship in 1971 and, in the process, earned many (mostly male) fans. *Playboy* magazine were among them, and asked her to display her, er, charms more explicitly. Ms Baugh turned down their offer, deciding that she'd rather stick to golf than appear on pages that might wind up stuck together.

74 Pro school

Preparing Brits for life on the US tour

IN 1973, THE BRITISH PGA OPENED A SCHOOL FOR GOLFERS. THE IDEA WAS THAT IT COULD PROVIDE PRACTICAL LESSONS FOR ANY PRO WHO WAS CONSIDERING PLAYING ON THE AMERICAN CIRCUIT.

THE COURSE INVOLVED TUITION IN THE SKILLS AND BUSINESS KNOWLEDGE REQUIRED BY TOUR PROS IN THE STATES PLUS EIGHT ROUNDS OF GOLF. THERE IS NO MENTION ON THE CURRICULUM OF BEING TAUGHT THE LANGUAGE, HOWEVER...

75 Golden Bear doubles up... again

Nicklaus bags another pair of majors

Hmm, that's the problem with majors, they're very moreish. Win one and you want another. By the mid-'70s, even winning one major a year didn't seem to be enough for Jack Nicklaus. (And you don't want to argue with a hungry bear…)

In 1975, he won both the USPGA and The Masters. It was the fourth time he had won two majors in a year. For a while though, The Masters was looking a bit touch and go. It came down to a dramatic shoot-out between Johnny Miller, Tom Weiskopf and Jack. With one hole left to play, Miller and Weiskopf were one shot behind Nicklaus. If either birdied the 18th hole, it would go to a play-off. Both had chances, but neither sank them, and the Bear got to put on the famous green jacket for a fifth time.

76 Brit pros make new deal

UK swingers follow US

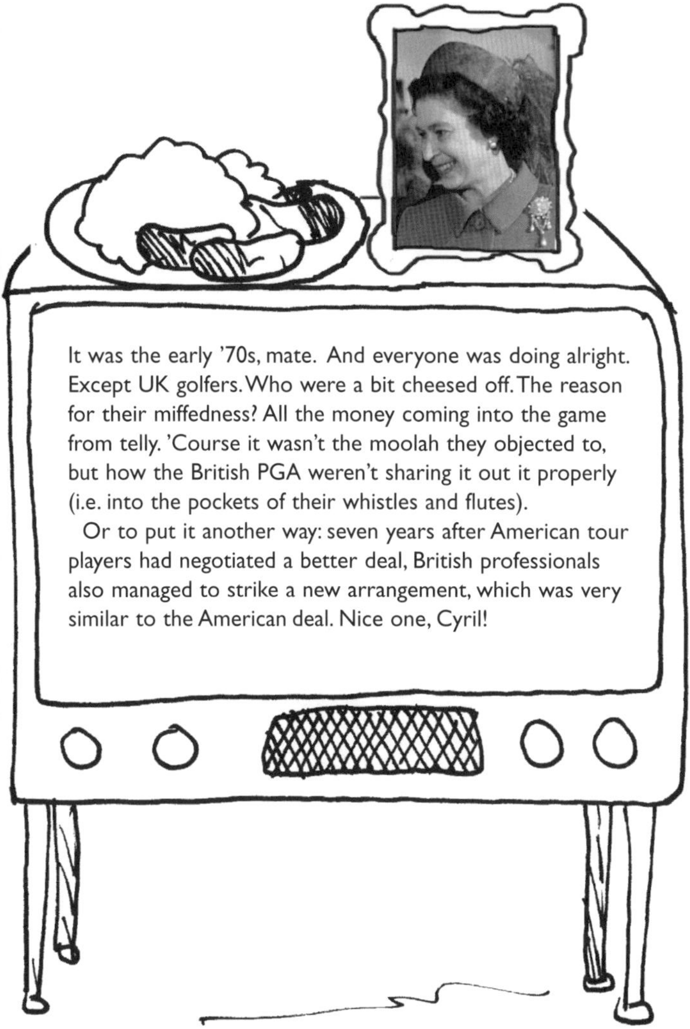

It was the early '70s, mate. And everyone was doing alright. Except UK golfers. Who were a bit cheesed off. The reason for their miffedness? All the money coming into the game from telly. 'Course it wasn't the moolah they objected to, but how the British PGA weren't sharing it out it properly (i.e. into the pockets of their whistles and flutes).

Or to put it another way: seven years after American tour players had negotiated a better deal, British professionals also managed to strike a new arrangement, which was very similar to the American deal. Nice one, Cyril!

77 Birdie blitz

Gary Player's masterful finish

At the 1978 Masters, Gary Player was most definitely not in the lead going into the last day as he trailed Hubert Green by seven strokes. Then, halfway through the final round, someone jokingly mentioned to Player that, hey, he needed "only" eight birdies to win The Masters. Player replied, possibly also joking: "Don't worry, I can get them." Nine birdies and a record-equalling round of 64 later, he was champion.

Coo!

78 Car park genius

Seve's park and drive...

Some players just don't like to make it too easy for themselves, do they?

Severiano Ballesteros was one such player. At once totally brilliant and completely erratic, spectators were never quite sure what would happen next with Seve. His 1979 British Open victory was a case in point.

Rarely the most accurate off the tee, Seve's drive ended up in the car park near the 16th hole on the final day. He still got down in two though, and The Open was in his grasp. It, um, drove the fans wild!

79 The trapeze artist

Super Seve hangs on to win the Masters

The circus is back in town! Yes, Seve was at it again at the 1980 Masters. Having built up a ten-stroke lead with just nine holes to play on the final day, he then proceeded to three-putt on the tenth, have a watery double-bogey at the 12th, another bogey at the 13th, where he went into the creek again, and then got himself into more trouble at the 14th when he was in the trees. One brilliiant shot saved his par there. Another earned him a birdie at the 15th and he eventually finished four ahead of the pack to earn his Green Jacket.

The Spaniard, who travelled everywhere with a trapeze (he hung upside down on it to relieve back pain), had, er, walked the tightrope yet again and survived.

80 Life begins at 40

The old bear doesn't need new tricks...

After losing out to Seve at The Masters and then failing to qualify at the Atlanta Classic, Jack Nicklaus started hearing rumours that it was time for the Golden Bear to retire and put on his slippers (assuming retired bears wear slippers...).

Naturally, the ol' grizzly was having none of it and roared back with victory in the 1980 US Open at Baltusrol. Grrr!

81 The 1001/1 shot

Tom Watson's takes a gamble

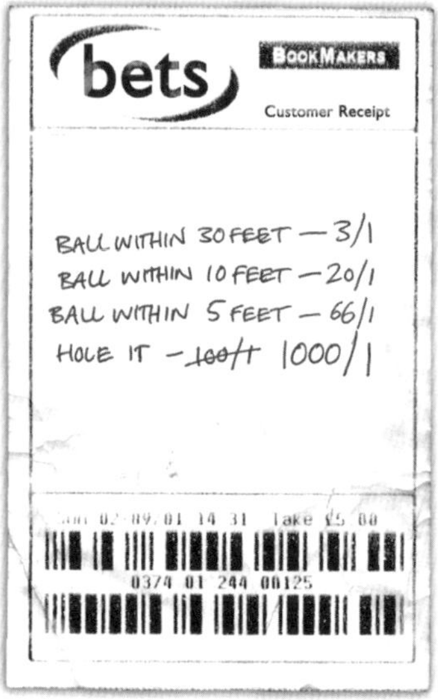

Sometimes, you just have to take a risk. "Risk it, for a biscuit" as one of our old teachers used to say. (Yes, clearly he was insane.)

With two holes to play in the 1982 US Open, Tom Watson knew he had to do something special. Two pars would mean a play-off, anything worse and the US Open would go to Jack Nicklaus.

When Watson's tee shot missed the green at the par three 17th, his odds of victory rapidly increased: fellow competitor Bill Rogers put it at 100–1. Nicklaus later said: "I'd have said 1000–1. At the very least, I thought I was in a play-off."

Shame neither of them put a bet on Watson before he chipped from the long, fluffy grass. A psychology graduate, he put himself in the right frame of mind, telling his caddie: "I'm not going to try and get close, I'm going to hole it."

He did, abandoning his normal reserve immediately afterwards to dance a jig on the green. He birdied again on the 17th to secure the trophy and went on to win the British Open that year, too. Dunno if he liked biscuits though…

82 Metal woods

They're not made of wood at all!

The '80s were a strange decade. Everything was just so confusing. Bad meant good. Greed was good, too. Style meant rolled-up sleeves and no socks. A wedge was a haircut. And woods weren't woods at all. They were metals!

Yes, golf club manufacturers were prime perpetrators in this world of confusion, especially when they started covering steel shafts in veneer to make them look like hickory shafts.

Alright, so maybe metals were just another technological advance in golf that we've all benefitted from and now we're all carrying drivers with names like "Big Bertha" and massive sweet spots, but, frankly, we feel lied to! Humpf! We're off to listen to *Rock Me Amadeus* – that always calms us down.

83 Bean flicker!

Hale Irwin's casually expensive miss

There are misses, and then there are misses. At the 14th hole, in the third round, of the 1983 British Open, Hale Irwin carelessly flicked at a two-inch putt and missed the ball completely.

Irwin ended up in a tie for second place with Andy Bean, just one stroke behind winner Tom Watson, making Irwin's flick one of the most expensive misses ever... Still, lucky it wasn't Irwin's fellow runner-up Andy Bean who'd flicked and missed, or we'd have done some dreadful headline and illustration…

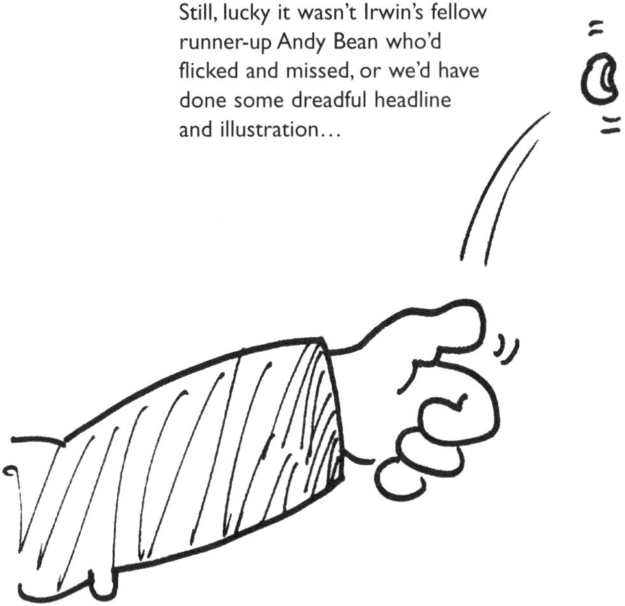

84 Video stars

Pros find new source of income

Back in the day when super-shiny DVDs were just a tinkle in a lab technician's eye, VHS ruled the world. The '80s saw nearly every household buy a video recorder and start taping whatever was on the other side.

Video stores also sprung up on every high street, although at first all you could rent were dodgy films that either starred Charles Bronson or were directed by Michael Winner. Or worse, involved both!

Into this glamorous world entered the humble golfer. A new avenue for generating income opened up to many pros with the rapid rise in popularity of the instructional video. Although, sadly, video didn't kill the average Joe's ability to forget everything they'd been taught, next time they went out and played a round.

85 Yip no more

Langer overcomes his putting woes

When watching a pro score metronomic par after par, it's easy to forget that they're human just like us. Which is probably why God invented the "yips" – the stuttering, nervy inability to putt smoothly that can affect the big names just as dramatically as the hobbyist. Famous golf journalist Henry Longhurst quit the game after he started suffering from them: "Once you've had 'em, you've got 'em," he claimed.

Hoping to disprove that theory was Bernhard Langer who, after battling with putting problems for many a tournament, adopted a cross-handed approach to shorter putts. It did the trick and the German's technique passed the ultimate test on the slicker-than-slick greens of Augusta at the 1985 Masters. Langer's nerve, and hands, stayed steady and he made just one three-putt during the entire tournament on his way to grabbing the famous Green Jacket for the first time.

"Yip-ee!!"

86 Water works

North's ball gets wet, Torrance's eyes get wetter

For the first time since 1957, and only the fourth time ever, America were parted from the Ryder Cup in 1985. Europe defeated the US 16-and-a-half to 11-and-a-half at The Belfry and Scot Sam Torrance won the singles match that took Europe over the line.

"I cried all the way from the 18th tee to the green," blubbed an emotional Torrance afterwards. "I knew I had won the Ryder Cup for us when Andy North drove into the water. I have dreamt of this all my life."

The victory was some (late) vindication for the decision to switch from a Britain and Ireland team to a European team back in 1979. Although the Americans still comfortably won it that year, it was fair to say that this time Europe had definitely made a splash…

87 Old Bear

The even-older-than-last-time Nicklaus does it again...

In 1986, Jack Nicklaus became the oldest winner of The Masters at the grand old age of 46. It was his sixth victory in the tournament and his 18th major in 24 years. His son Jack Jr. caddied for him at the tournament, transporting all his clubs and, of course, carrying his walking stick… (only kidding, Jack).

88 Par for the course

18 pars wins Faldo the British Open

Sometimes the trick to a good round isn't about the spectacular birdie but the routine **PAR**. Consistency is the key, as Nick Faldo proved in the final round of the 1987 British Open at Muirfield when he won the tournament by hitting **PAR** after **PAR** after **PAR**. Yes, he hit **PAR** at the first, **PAR** at the 18th and **PAR** at every hole in between.

It's actually pretty difficult to keep hitting **PAR**. And certainly to hit **PAR** 18 times is very hard (hell, we're struggling to hit **PAR** 18 times on a page).

By the time Faldo hit the back nine (of course having hit **PAR** on all of the first nine), he was three shots behind the leader Paul Azinger. But Azinger bogied the tenth (Faldo hit **PAR**), then Azinger three putted the 11th (Faldo scored… yes, that's right, **PAR**!)

There was now just one shot in it, which is how it stayed all the way to the 17th as both players hit **PAR** for five straight holes. Then Azinger bogied the 17th (guess who'd hit **PAR** there?) and it was all square. Faldo reached the 18th at Muirfield first and, surprising no-one, hit **PAR**.

Now it was all down to Azinger. He needed a birdie to win and a **PAR** to tie, but his final drive left him 200 yards from the green. Then a bunker beckoned and it was all over. He bogied and Faldo had won thanks to his **PAR** round. Phew!

89 Tree-mendous!

Woosie's stroke of luck

The Ryder Cup's a team game, so it's important that everyone – player, fan and, er, tree does their duty. Such was the case in the 1987 Ryder Cup, where the European team were bidding for their first-ever victory on American soil.

Ian Woosnam and Nick Faldo needed something special to beat Lanny Wadkins and Larry Mize in the fourballs and they got it. At the 11th, Woosnam hit a shot wide, but it struck a tree and dropped onto the green where he holed for an eagle.

Europe proceeded to secure an historic victory by 15 points to 13. Wood you believe it!

90 Green bugged out

Hubert seeks vengeance on TV man

When you're watching golf on the telly, you don't really think about all the technicians and cameramen running all over the course (well, we don't anyway...).

However, at the 1988 US Open, Hubert Green thought about it. He thought about it a lot. Mainly because a television crew's buggy had driven over his ball.

Hubert demanded justice and sought out the authorities advice:

"I want a ruling," he declared. "I need to know which club to hit this guy with."

Curiously, there are no guidelines in the coaching manual covering the attacking of TV personnel, but we'd probably suggest using a nine iron.

91 Two much?

Golf fashion. A (very) short history

The 1989 USPGA was won by Payne Stewart, a man whose flamboyant dress sense wasn't to everyone's taste but whose "style" does provide a handy entry into a discourse on golf fashion. The words "golf" and "fashion" probably shouldn't ever be combined as they appear diametrically opposed. Naturally though, that won't stop us pontificating about it.

Stewart's clothing contract specified that he appeared in sets of plus twos and tops in the club

colours of the various local American football teams.

Other joys over the years included ankle-length skirts for women (now replaced with more sensible looking shorts), tail coats for men, buckled shoes, checkerboard trousers, garish socks and Scottish knitwear with diamond patterns.

The scariest thing though is that golfers still dress far better than those dreadful people who write books about golf...

92 Bottoms up

Champ Faldo pays, um, hearty tribute to the press

After his 1989 Masters win, Nick Faldo made it a double in 1990, winning The Masters again and then the British Open.

The obsessive Brit was much admired for his metronomic efficiency on the fairways and greens, but perhaps less so off the course where he maintained a somewhat strained relationship with the media. As he would later say after his 1992 British Open victory: "I thank the press from the heart of my, well, bottom."

Our guess is that the feeling may well have been mutual…

93 Club record

World's most expensive clubs go under the hammer

Golfing memorabilia is now big business. In fact, one day this very book you hold in your hands will probably be worth an absolute fortune (so perhaps you'd better go out and buy another copy, just to be on the safe side...).

However, as we haven't yet come up for auction, the record fee paid remains the £627,000 spent at a Sotheby auction on the world's most expensive collection of golf clubs. All 23 of the clubs were used by a former Open champion between 1860 and 1930, making them highly collectible.

But still, wouldn't you rather have a good book? Oh, that's just us, then.

94 Long-distance driver

The emergence of John "Wild Thing" Daly

Just 48 hours before the 1991 USPGA got underway, the eventual winner was more than a seven-hour drive away. John Daly was at one stage a ninth alternate for the event but, after a series of late exits, decided to take a chance and make the trip from Dardanelle, Arkansas, to Crooked Stick, Carmel, Indiana. By the time he arrived, Nick Price had departed because his wife was about to go into labour and Daly was in.

Four rounds of long drives ("I don't even drive that far when I go on vacation," observed Raymond Floyd) and accurate putts later, Daly was champion. The "Wild Thing" went on to be a crowd favourite, the authorities' nightmare and a tabloid editor's dream with his erratic play and behaviour. Whatever tales of domestic squabbles and alcohol-fuelled antics emerge, however, he still hits a ball a very, very long way…

95 Bad buzz

Fly-on-the-wall documentary empties boardroom

Golf, it has to be said, has not always been the most politically correct of sports. Racism and sexism, among other "isms", have reared their ugly heads a fair few times along the sport's history as some of the rather cantankerous old buggers in charge buried their heads in bunkers and tried to ignore the modern world.

In recent years, things have improved somewhat, but scandals never seem to be too far beneath the surface. Which is probably why, in 1994, a British TV company decided to make a fly-on-the-wall documentary about Northwood Golf Club in North London.

If the TV crew were hoping for some juicy tidbits, they got their wish. The broadcast of the programme resulted in the entire board promptly resigning. Members of the club felt that the documentary had made them a laughing stock after it indicated that the club was a stronghold for male chauvinism and Freemasonry.

Strangely, none of the former board went on to become reality TV "celebrities". For which small mercies, we should be thankful.

96 D'oh!

Ryder Cup not quite as popular as first thought...

Surveys can be wonderful things. Send a bunch of people out with clipboards, get 'em to ask loads of daft questions, collate all the answers and you'll always come up some juicy morsels of trivia. For example, 19 per cent of teachers actually want to be professional wrestlers, 46 per cent of teenagers secretly like country music and 97 per cent of women admit they would never sleep with the writer of a reduced history of golf (anyone have the phone numbers for the other three per cent?)

Okay, we might have made some of those up (except the last one), but when an American magazine poll asked what sport the Ryder Cup is associated with, only 12 per cent replied golf. Over 37 per cent thought it was actually something to do with horse racing. Which may explain Europe's recent success rate…

97 Elephants, sharks and tigers!

Why 1996 was a golfing jungle...

The genteel greeens of the golfer's world are not often compared to a wild jungle, but perhaps that's simply because the kind of book to make such absurd comparisons did not exist. Until now!

Yes, dear reader, as far as we're concerned, 1996 was definitely golf's Year of the Jungle.

Consider the evidence: first of all there was Nick Faldo shark-baiting. The Brit had a whale of a time against Greg "Great White Shark" Norman at The Masters. Faldo eventually triumphed, while others struggled to cope with the wildly undulating greens.

Mark Roe summed up the

thoughts of many players when he commented: "The greens look as though elephants have been buried every ten feet."

1996 was also the year Tiger Woods was crowned US Amateur Champion for an unprecedented third time. He turned pro straight afterwards, signing a decidedly un-amateur series of sponsorship deals worth over $10 million. Within a year he became the youngest Masters champion ever.

So, there you have it: 1996 saw elephants, tigers and sharks – and anyone who wishes to point out that sharks don't live in jungles can just take a hike.

98 Old dog comes good

Mark O'Meara's shows he hasn't lost his bark

Despite the emergence of several young pups, such as Justin Leonard and Tiger Woods, it was an old dog (well, 41-year-old Mark O'Meara) who had his day at the 1998 US Masters.

Woods, the '97 winner, and Leonard, the previous year's British Open victor, could only look on as O'Meara made two birdies at the last three at Augusta to earn the coveted Green Jacket (and trouser a handy $576,000).

As Woods helped O'Meara put the jacket on, the oldster joked: "Don't hold it so high – at 41, I can't get my arms up there!"

But there didn't seem to be much wrong with his arms a few months later at the British Open. Again, the early headlines were made by another youngster – this time, a puppy called Justin Rose – the 17-year-old amateur doing spectacularly well in his first major. But, come trophy time, O'Meara was ahead of the pack again to ensure he had the last, er, woof.

99 Mickleson's marathon win

Rain stops play… for seven months!

Golf is hardly the speediest of games. Nothing's decided in 90 minutes, or often, in a day. Nonetheless, spectators usually only have to sit around for four days to see a result.

Not so for the poor unfortunates who'd settled in to watch the AT&T at Pebble Beach in 1998.

Although the tournament began in January, heavy rain meant that the final round couldn't be played. It was eventually rescheduled for August. Those patient spectators who remained (because we're sure they didn't go home in the interim…) were witness to a Phil Mickleson victory. Beard-tastic!

100 Frenchman loses le plot!

Jan Van de Velde's watery misery

There have been plenty of nearly men in golf but few have come so close to glory and thrown it away more stupidly, and, indeed, wetly, than Jean Van de Velde. In 1999, on the verge of becoming the first Frenchman since Arnaud Massey to win the British Open, Van de Velde managed to throw it all away. He started the final day five shots ahead of the pack and reached the final hole needing to shoot just a six to win The Open.

Having landed in short grass near the 17th fairway, two cautious irons would have secured a five. Instead, the Frenchman took out a two-iron, hit a grandstand and landed in long grass. From there he hit his ball into the watery burn, tried to splash out (unsuccessfully) and eventually signed for a seven. He lost the subsequent three-way play-off to qualifier Paul Lawrie, with Justin Leonard finishing second. Eau dear!

101 Laser eyes

Tiger Woods gets eye surgery... and a lot of trophies

In 1999 Tiger Woods had laser eye surgery. This wasn't some elaborate operation to give him super powers. It was just a run-of-the-mill-optician-type gig. Well, that's his story anyway.

Consider the evidence: within a year of this so-called "routine surgery", Woods won nine times on the USPGA Tour – the most for 50 years – including three of the four major championships. In doing so, he produced a new set of records so bewildering that even the most acute insomnia sufferer would be aroused.

Holder of the record lowest score in all four majors, his 15-stroke victory at the US Open was the largest winning margin at a major, beating by two the previous record set by Old Tom Morris in the Open in 1862. Woods' 19-under-par total at St Andrews was the lowest for any major, and in so doing he avoided all 120 of St Andrews notorious bunkers. By season's end he'd banked prize money to the value of some $10 million!

Our verdict? He has superpowers. Another case solved.

102 Woosie gets Byrned

The caddie who couldn't, er, addie...

Hey kids, counting's great isn't it? One, two, three... see how easy it is! Go on, you have a go! Well done. But, of course you know who's not so good at counting – Ian Woosnam's ex-caddie, Myles Byrne. Hapless Myles managed to miscount how many clubs were in Woosnam's bag when the Welshman was in contention going into the last round of the 2001 British Open. And Woosie felt decidedly woozy when he was penalised two strokes for having a club too many, thus scuppering his title chances.

Myles is no longer a caddie – he works in construction. Which is a bit like playing with building blocks. That sounds like fun, doesn't it kids?

Today's story was brought to you by the letters S, T, U, P, I and D...

103 The full Monty

The merits of Colin Montgomerie

Colin Montgomerie used to pride himself on the fact that he never had to practise hitting the ball straight, so naturally did it come to him. Indeed, fellow pro Steve Elkington once rather vividly commented: "Colin's the only guy who could drive it up a gnat's ass every hole."

Gnat's everywhere were not amused. Americans weren't too keen on him either, labelling him "Mrs Doubtfire". Although, as far as we're aware, no cross-dressing nanny ever won seven European Orders of Merit, as Monty did. He's also a Ryder Cup player par excellence, never more so than in 2002 when, on the back of a pretty miserable year, he became Europe's hero at The Belfry as the top scorer on either side as Europe claimed victory. Americans, and gnats, remain nervous around him.

104 No girls!

Augusta's unfeminine policy

In 2002, Augusta National Golf Club proudly unveiled its revamped course in time for The Masters. Unfortunately, the club didn't revamp its membership policy to admit women.

Funnily enough, this didn't go down too well with women. Or some men, either.

But Augusta refuses to budge. It is a place of tradition and, er, painted greens and dyed creeks. Chairman William "Hootie" Johnson, and Martha Burk, the chairwoman of the National Council of Women's Organizations have been battling it out ever since.

So, the war of the sexes goes on. But, if nobody minds, we'll continue to hide behind the sofa until it's all over.

105 Girls allowed!

Star Sorenstam takes on the men

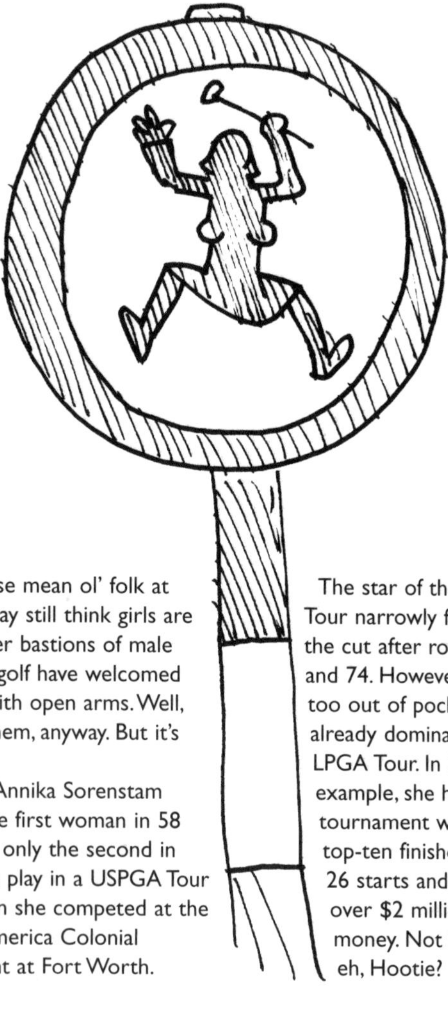

While those mean ol' folk at Augusta may still think girls are yucky, other bastions of male American golf have welcomed them all with open arms. Well, some of them, anyway. But it's a start.

In 2003, Annika Sorenstam became the first woman in 58 years (and only the second in history) to play in a USPGA Tour event when she competed at the Bank of America Colonial tournament at Fort Worth.

The star of the Women's Tour narrowly failed to make the cut after rounds of 70 and 74. However, she wasn't too out of pocket as she'd already dominated the LPGA Tour. In 2001, for example, she had eight tournament wins, 20 top-ten finishes from 26 starts and banked over $2 million in prize money. Not bad for a girl, eh, Hootie?

106 Tiger tamed

Woods, er, Singhs the blues

After five years standing on top of the world (obviously, not literally…) Tiger Woods' reign as world number one was ended when he was replaced at the top of the players' table (again, not literally a table) by Vijay Singh.

In 2004, Singh's name became synonymous with winning. In fact, in Hindi, "Vijay" quite literally means "victory".

Which is pretty apt, as Fijian Vijay won nine tournaments during the year, including the USPGA Championship. He also became the first player to quite literally "pocket" $10 million in a season.

In a decision that shocked no-one, he was also named USPGA Player of the Year.

Tiger was as sick as a parrot, or, quite literally, a sick tiger.

107 No sleep 'til Heathrow

Europe celebrates another Ryder Cup victory

Europe continued their recent habit of winning Ryder Cups by, er, winning the Ryder Cup at Oakland Hills in 2004. A delighted Darren Clarke said afterwards that as everyone was so delighted, not only would the players party all night, they would continue the party on the plane home the next day: "There'll be no sleep, just a partying plane."

There was good cause for celebration. With their victory, Europe made it four wins out of the last five of the biennial matches against the United States and in the process handed America their heaviest defeat in the competition's 77-year history, 18-and-a-half to 9-and-a-half. In fact, some said it was, ahem, plane sailing.

108 What next for golf?

That is the big question...

Golf's come a long way since the days of *chole* and *kolven* but what lies ahead? Obviously, we have no idea. But that won't stop us speculating wildly. For a start, technology seems to be taking an ever-tighter grip on proceedings. Clubs are being developed that hit further and straighter than ever before and there are balls that practically seek out the hole. Golf courses are already being lengthened to cope. Alarmists, and people who like to speculate wildly, are growing concerned that courses will have to get longer and more fiendish. Meanwhile, absurdists, and people who like to speculate wildly, reckon that if this continues, courses will eventually take up whole cities. Which will leave no room for the population. They'll have to live on top of mountains. And authors of reduced histories, in order to maintain their perspective, will have to occupy floating kingdoms, hundreds of feet above the populace, where they'll probably be adored by all – but particularly by alarmists, aburdists and people who like to speculate wildly.

THE 19TH HOLE